H.P. LOVECRAFT:

Fungi from Yuggoth: The Sonnet Cycle
Contextualized with a Selection of Other Lovecraft Poems

H.P. LOVECRAFT

FUNGI FROM YUGGOTH – THE SONNET CYCLE:

Contextualized with a Selection of Other Lovecraft Poems

A Pulp-Lit Annotated Edition

By H.P. LOVECRAFT

Edited and Annotated by FINN J.D. JOHN

Pulp-Lit

PRODUCTIONS

Corvallis • Oregon

Cover art: Front cover based on the unsigned illustrations
on page 6-7 of *Startling Mysteries* magazine, April 1940,
illustrating *Flesh for the Devil's Piper* by Wayne Rogers. Cover
design by Fiona Mac Daibheid.

Pulp-Lit Productions
P.O. Box 77
Corvallis, Oregon

http://pulp-lit.com

CONTENTS

Foreword.

Howard Phillips Lovecraft wrote his most well-known work of poetry—*Fungi from Yuggoth*—in a one-week burst of creative energy that started very late in 1929, centered precisely around New Year's Day.

It had been a good year for the poet, if not for his weird-fiction fans; in fact, 1929 had been something of a bye year for them. It was the only year between 1917 and 1936 in which he actually added nothing at all to his weird-fiction canon. He had, the year before, belted out a tale that might have actually been his best work to date: *The Dunwitch Horror*. He'd followed that up with several big ghostwriting jobs, and by the end of the year he was feeling prosperous enough to do some low-budget traveling. He also started the first of several beefy travelogues, written purely for his own enjoyment.

And it was the end of that year—apparently also purely for his own enjoyment—that he turned his attention back to a writing style that he'd neglected a bit over the previous half-dozen years: Poetry.

There had been a time when Lovecraft had considered himself primarily a poet. In the years after high school, before he got involved with the amateur-press movement and rediscovered his talent for weird fiction, he wrote almost nothing but poetry—and, of course, letters; Lovecraft very likely was the most prolific epistolarian of the 20th century.

His poetry at that time was unfashionable by design. As a stylistic decision, Lovecraft shunned the more modern forms of poetry, writing primarily in formats that were popular in the 1700s (and sometimes in the language of that Georgian era as well). So, although he published plenty of it in friends' amateur-press journals, he primarily worked for his own enjoyment.

When Lovecraft's ghostwriting and weird-fiction writing output ramped up in 1917, his poetic output started to slow down, and the early 1920s were fairly lean years. Lovecraft was focusing on other things. Between 1921 and 1928, Lovecraft wrote fewer than 60 poems, according to S.T. Joshi in *The Ancient Track: The Complete Poetical Works of H.P. Lovecraft*. This sounds like a beefy number, but it comes to fewer than 10 poems per year, and it's a fraction of what his output had been throughout the 1910s.

It appears that Lovecraft had simply moved away from poetry as a literary form during the time he was striving to make a name for himself as a new kind of weird-fictioneer. But then had come that dreadful interlude in New York, stranded away from his beloved Providence home and surrounded by people he didn't understand. So when he returned to Providence in 1926 and settled into a life that seemed rather a lot like retirement, after he had settled back into the town and written some of the finest stories of his career, he naturally turned back to poetry—the primary form of creative expression in his youth.

It was November of 1929 that he really got into it. Among the poetical works to come off his pen that month were *The Outpost, The Ancient Track*—and, at the very end of the year, in a weeklong outburst that precisely bracketed the end of the old decade and the start of the new, *Fungi from Yuggoth*.

Fungi *from Yuggoth* is a sequence of 36 sonnets. Lovecraft wrote them all at once during that productive week, so they are usually treated as a sonnet cycle—that is, a group of sonnets all clustered around a particular topic or theme, intended to be readable both individually and as a group—rather like one of the "rock-opera" albums that rose to popularity several dozen years ago in the music world. However, not all scholars agree that *Fungi from Yuggoth* qualifies as a cycle; some of the sonnets in it seem to carry a narrative forward from poem to poem, especially the first three; but most do not.

I'll leave it to you to decide if *Fungi from Yuggoth* is a "real" cycle or not. Should the question interest you, it will not be difficult to look into; there's been quite a lot of scholarship done on *Fungi from Yuggoth*, more than any other of Lovecraft's poems.

Although this collection is primarily focused on *Fungi from Yuggoth*, several other of Lovecraft's poems have been selected to add context to it, so that the sonnets' place in Lovecraft's literary career can be better understood and visualized.

We're starting out with four poems selected from Lovecraft's early work—formal works with strong, vigorous structure and robust, often dactylic meter:

Unda; or, The Bride of the Sea (1915): One of the longer works of Lovecraft's youth, penned when he was 25 years old.

Untitled (a Georgian drinking-song) (1917): This rollicking macabre drinking song appears in one of Lovecraft's first weird-fiction stories: *The Tomb*. He appears to have written the poem specifically for that story.

Nemesis (1918): An excerpt from this poem appears in Lovecraft's 1919 short story Beyond the Wall of Sleep.

Psychopompos: A Tale in Rhyme (1919): This appears to have been an experimentation with a sort of fusion format—a weird tale told in the formal verse with which Lovecraft was now so familiar.

Next we move on to the late-1929 re-flowering of Lovecraft's poetry. There are not many of them, but you will immediately notice the difference in their evocative poise and power:

The Outpost and *The Ancient Track* (1929): A pair of short poems—stylistically similar, but not intended as a matched set—crafted in a style similar to his works of old , but noticeably more polished and evocative.

Fungi from Yuggoth (1929-1930): The cycle of 36 sonnets which is the centerpiece of this book. We will briefly discuss this set, the crown jewel of Lovecraft's poetical output, just before it is presented.

Finally, we finish this collection off with a brace of short poems that Lovecraft wrote in 1936—the year before his death: *In a Sequester'd Providence Churchyard where Once Poe Walked*, and *To Clark Ashton Smith, Esq., upon his Phantastick Tales, Verses, Pictures and Sculptures.*

Both these poems are quite short—sonnets, in fact. Yet they represent the lion's share of Lovecraft's total output in the seven years of his life following publication of *Fungi from Yuggoth*. It was almost as if Lovecraft had wanted to get serious poetry out of his system so that he could focus on other endeavors; after completion of *Fungi from Yuggoth*, for the rest of his life Lovecraft would create poetry only occasionally, and usually in commemoration of a special occasion such as Christmas, or as a special tribute to a good friend.

—FINN J.D. JOHN

Part I.

Early poetry: 1915-1919.

The following four poems have been chosen as a good representation of the state of Lovecraft's artistry in his early years, during the time when he considered himself primarily a poet. The first two do an excellent job of showcasing Lovecraft's wit and dry sense of humor; the third, *Nemesis*, is one of his best cosmic-horror poems; and the final poem, *Psychopompos*, appears to be a successful experiment in a sort of modern twist on epic poetry.

Unda; or, The Bride of the Sea.

A Dull, Dark, Drear, Dactylic Delirium
in Sixteen Silly, Senseless, Sickly Stanzas.

"Ego, canus, lunam cano."
—Maevius Bavianus.

Black loom the crags of the uplands behind me;
Dark are the sands of the far-stretching shore.
Dim are the pathways and rocks that remind me
Sadly of years in the lost nevermore.

Soft laps the ocean on wave-polish'd boulder;
Sweet is the sound and familiar to me.
Here, with her head gently bent to my shoulder,
Walk'd I with Unda, the Bride of the Sea.

Bright was the morn of my youth when I met her,
Sweet as the breeze that blew in o'er the brine.
Swift was I captur'd in Love's strongest fetter,
Glad to be hers, and she glad to be mine.

Never a question ask'd I where she wander'd,
Never a question ask'd she of my birth:
Happy as children, we thought not nor ponder'd,
Glad with the bounty of ocean and earth.

Once when the moonlight play'd soft 'mid the billows,
High on the cliff o'er the waters we stood,
Bound was her hair with a garland of willows,
Pluck'd by the fount in the bird-haunted wood.

Strangely she gaz'd on the surges beneath her,
Charm'd by the sound or entranc'd by the light.
Then did the waves a wild aspect bequeath her,
Stern as the ocean and weird as the night.

Coldly she left me, astonish'd and weeping,
Standing alone 'mid the regions she bless'd:
Down, ever downward, half gliding, half creeping,
Stole the sweet Unda in oceanward quest.

Calm grew the sea, and tumultuous beating
Turn'd to a ripple, as Unda the fair
Trod the wet sands in affectionate greeting,
Beckon'd to me, and no longer was there!

Long did I pace by the banks where she vanish'd:
High climb'd the moon, and descended again.
Grey broke the dawn till the sad night was banish'd,
Still ach'd my soul with its infinite pain.

All the wide world have I search'd for my darling,
Scour'd the far deserts and sail'd distant seas.
Once on the wave while the tempest was snarling,
Flash'd a fair face that brought quiet and ease.

Ever in restlessness onward I stumble,
Seeking and pining, scarce heeding my way.
Now have I stray'd where the wide waters rumble,
Back to the scene of the lost yesterday.

Lo! the red moon from the ocean's low hazes
Rises in ominous grandeur to view.
Strange is its face as my tortur'd eye gazes
O'er the vast reaches of sparkle and blue.

Straight from the moon to the shore where I'm sighing
Grows a bright bridge, made of wavelets and beams.
Frail may it be, yet how simple the trying;
Wand'ring from earth to the orb of sweet dreams.

What is yon face in the moonlight appearing;
Have I at last found the maiden that fled?
Out on the beam-bridge my footsteps are nearing
Her whose sweet beckoning hastens my tread.

Currents surround me, and drowsily swaying,
Far on the moon-path I seek the sweet face.
Eagerly hasting, half panting, half praying,
Forward I reach for the vision of grace.

Murmuring waters about me are closing,
Soft the sweet vision advances to me:
Done are my trials; my heart is reposing
Safe with my Unda, the Bride of the Sea.

Epilogue

As the rash fool, a prey of Unda's art,
Drown thro' the passion of his fever'd heart,
So are our youth, inflam'd by tempters fair,
Bereft of reason and the manly air.
How sad the sight of Strephon's virile grace
Turn'd to confusion at his Chloë's face,
And e'er Pelides, dear to Grecian eyes,
Sulking for loss of his thrice-cherish'd prize.
Brothers, attend! If cares too sharply vex,
Gain rest by shunning the destructive sex!

Untitled Drinking-Song.

"One morning at breakfast I came close to disaster by declaiming in palpably liquorish accents an effusion of eighteenth-century Baccanalian mirth; a bit of Georgian playfulness never recorded in a book, which ran something like this:"

—*From* The Tomb.

Come hither, my lads, with your tankards of ale,
And drink to the present before it shall fail;
Pile each on your platter a mountain of beef,
For 'tis eating and drinking that bring us relief:
    So fill up your glass,
    So life will soon pass;
When you're dead ye'll ne'er drink to your king or
your lass!

Anacreon had a red nose, so they say;
But what's a red nose if ye're happy and gay?
Gad split me! I'd rather be red whilst I'm here,
Than white as a lily—and dead half a year!
    So Betty, my miss,
    Come give me kiss;
In hell there's no innkeeper's daughter like this!

Young Harry, propp'd up just as straight as he's able,
Will soon lose his wig and slip under the table;
But fill up your goblets and pass 'em around—
Better under the table than under the ground!
    So revel and chaff
    As ye thirstily quaff:
Under six feet of dirt 'tis less easy to laugh!

The fiend strike me blue! I'm scarce able to walk,
And damn me if I can stand upright or talk!
Here, landlord, bid Betty to summon a chair;
I'll try home for a while, for my wife is not there!
    So lend me a hand;
    I'm not able to stand,
But I'm gay whilst I linger on top of the land!

Nemesis.

Thro' the ghoul-guarded gateways of slumber,
Past the wan-moon'd abysses of night,
I have liv'd o'er my lives without number,
I have sounded all things with my sight;
And I struggle and shriek ere the daybreak,
      being driven to madness with fright.

I have whirl'd with the earth at the dawning,
When the sky was a vaporous flame;
I have seen the dark universe yawning,
Where the black planets roll without aim;
Where they roll in their horror unheeded,
      without knowledge or lustre or name.

I had drifted o'er seas without ending,
Under sinister grey-clouded skies
That the many-fork'd lightning is rending,
That resound with hysterical cries;
With the moans of invisible daemons
    that out of the green waters rise.

I have plung'd like a deer thro' the arches
Of the hoary primoridal grove,
Where the oaks feel the presence that marches
And stalks on where no spirit dares rove;
And I flee from a thing that surrounds me,
    and leers thro' dead branches above.

I have stumbled by cave-ridden mountains
That rise barren and bleak from the plain,
I have drunk of the fog-foetid fountains
That ooze down to the marsh and the main;
And in hot cursed tarns I have seen things
    I care not to gaze on again.

I have scann'd the vast ivy-clad palace,
I have trod its untenanted hall,
Where the moon writhing up from the valleys
Shews the tapestried things on the wall;
Strange figures discordantly woven,
    which I cannot endure to recall.

I have peer'd from the casement in wonder
At the mouldering meadows around,
At the many-roof'd village laid under
The curse of a grave-girdled ground;
And from rows of white urn-carven marble
     I listen intently for sound.

I have haunted the tombs of the ages,
I have flown on the pinions of fear
Where the smoke-belching Erebus rages,
Where the jokulls loom snow-clad and drear:
And in realms where the sun of the desert
     consumes what it never can cheer.

I was old when the Pharaohs first mounted
The jewel-deck'd throne by the Nile;
I was old in those epochs uncounted
When I, and I only, was vile;
And Man, yet untainted and happy,
     dwelt in bliss on the far Arctic isle.

Oh, great was the sin of my spirit,
And great is the reach of its doom;
Not the pity of Heaven can cheer it,
Nor can respite be found in the tomb:
Down the infinite aeons come beating
     the wings of unmerciful gloom.

Thro' the ghoul-guarded gateways of slumber,
Past the wan-moon'd abysses of night,
I have liv'd o'er my lives without number,
I have sounded all things with my sight;
And I struggle and shriek ere the daybreak,
    being driven to madness with fright.

Psychopompos: A Tale in Rhyme.

I am He who howls in the night;
    I am He who moans in the snow;
I am He who hath never seen light;
    I am He who mounts from below.

My car is the car of Death;
    My wings are the wings of dread;
My breath is the north wind's breath;
    My prey are the cold and the dead.

In old Auvergne, when schools were poor and few,
And peasants fancy'd what they scarcely knew,
When lords and gentry shunn'd their Monarch's throne
For solitary castles of their own,

There dwelt a man of rank, whose fortress stood
In the hush'd twilight of a hoary wood.
De Blois his name; his lineage high and vast,
A proud memorial of an honour'd past;
But curious swains would whisper now and then
That Sieur De Blois was not as other men.
In person dark and lean, with glossy hair,
And gleaming teeth that he would often bare,
With piercing eye, and stealthy roving glance,
And tongue that clipt the soft, sweet speech of France;
The Sieur was little lov'd and seldom seen,
So close he kept within his own demesne.

The castle servants, few, discreet, and old,
Full many a tale of strangeness might have told;
But bow'd with years, they rarely left the door
Wherein their sires and grandsires serv'd before.
Thus gossip rose, as gossip rises best,
When mystery imparts a keener zest;
Seclusion oft the poison tongue attracts,
And scandal prospers on a dearth of facts.
'Twas said, the Sieur had more than once been spy'd
Alone at midnight by the river's side,
With aspect so uncouth, and gaze so strange,
That rustics cross'd themselves to see the change;
Yet none, when press'd, could clearly say or know
Just what it was, or why they trembled so.
De Blois, as rumour whisper'd, fear'd to pray,
Nor us'd his chapel on the Sabbath day;
Howe'er this may have been, 'twas known at least
His household had no chaplain, monk, or priest.

But if the Master liv'd in dubious fame,
Twice fear'd and hated was his noble Dame;
As dark as he, in features wild and proud,
And with a weird supernal grace endow'd,
The haughty mistress scorn'd the rural train
Who sought to learn her source, but sought in vain.
Old women call'd her eyes too bright by half,
And nervous children shiver'd at her laugh;
Richard, the dwarf (whose word had little weight),
Vow'd she was like a serpent in her gait,
Whilst ancient Pierre (the aged often err)
Laid all her husband's mystery to her.
Still more absurd were those odd mutter'd things
That calumny to curious list'ners brings;
Those subtle slanders, told with downcast face,
And muffled voice—those tales no man may trace;
Tales that the faith of old wives can command,
Tho' always heard at sixth or seventh hand.
Thus village legend darkly would imply
That Dame De Blois possess'd an evil eye;
Or going further, furtively suggest
A lurking spark of sorcery in her breast;
Old Mère Allard (herself half witch) once said
The lady's glance work'd strangely on the dead.
So liv'd the pair, like many another two
That shun the crowd, and shrink from public view.
They scorn'd the doubts by ev'ry peasant shewn,
And ask'd but one thing—to be let alone!

'Twas Candlemas, the dreariest time of year,
With fall long gone, and spring too far to cheer,

When little Jean, the bailiff's son and heir,
Fell sick and threw the doctors in despair.
A child so stout and strong that few would think
An hour might carry him to death's dark brink,
Yet pale he lay, tho' hidden was the cause,
And Galens search'd in vain thro' Nature's laws.
But stricken sadness could not quite suppress
The roving thought, or wrinkled grandam's guess:
Tho' spoke by stealth, 'twas known to half a score
That Dame De Blois rode by the day before;
She had (they said) with glances weird and wild
Paus'd by the gate to view the prattling child,
Nor did they like the smile which seem'd to trace
New lines of evil on her proud, dark face.
These things they whisper'd, when the mother's cry
Told of the end—the gentle soul gone by;
In genuine grief the kindly watcher wept,
Whilst the lov'd babe with saints and angels slept.
The village priest his simple rites went thro',
And good Michel nail'd up the box of yew;
Around the corpse the holy candles burn'd,
The mourners sighed, the parents dumbly yearn'd.
Then one by one each sought his humble bed,
And left the lonely mother with her dead.

Late in the night it was, when o'er the vale
The storm-king swept with pandemoniac gale;
Deep pil'd the cruel snow, yet strange to tell,
The lightning sputter'd while the white flakes fell;
A hideous presence seem'd abroad to steal,
And terror sounded in the thunder's peal.

Within the house of grief the tapers glow'd
Whilst the poor mother bow'd beneath her load;
Her salty eyes too tired now to weep,
Too pain'd to see, too sad to close in sleep.
The clock struck three, above the tempest heard,
When something near the lifeless infant stirr'd;
Some slipp'ry thing, that flopp'd in awkward way,
And climb'd the table where the coffin lay;
With scaly convolutions strove to find
The cold, still clay that death had left behind.
The nodding mother hears—starts broad awake—
Empower'd to reason, yet too stunn'd to shake;
The pois'nous thing she sees, and nimbly foils
The ghoulish purpose of the quiv'ring coils:
With ready axe the serpent's head she cleaves,
And thrills with savage triumph whilst she grieves.
The injur'd reptile hissing glides from sight,
And hides its cloven carcass in the night.

The weeks slipp'd by, and gossip's tongue began
To call the Sieur De Blois an alter'd man;
With curious mien he oft would pace along
The village street, and eye the gaping throng.
Yet whilst he shew'd himself as ne'er before,
His wild-eyed lady was observ'd no more.
In course of time, 'twas scarce thought odd or ill
That he his ears with village lore should fill;
Nor was the town with special rumour rife
When he sought out the bailiff and his wife:
Their tale of sorrow, with its ghastly end,
Was told, indeed, by ev'ry wond'ring friend.

25

The Sieur heard all, and low'ring rode away,
Nor was he seen again for many a day.

When vernal sunshine shed its cheering glow,
And genial zephyrs blew away the snow,
To frighten'd swains a horror was reveal'd
In the damp herbage of a melting field.
There (half preserv'd by winter's frigid bed)
Lay the dark Dame De Blois, untimely dead;
By some assassin's stroke most foully slain,
Her shapely brow and temples cleft in twain.
Reluctant hands the dismal burden bore
To the stone arches of the husband's door,
Where silent serfs the ghastly thing receiv'd,
Trembling with fright, but less amaz'd than griev'd;
The Sieur his dame beheld with blazing eyes,
And shook with anger, more than with surprise.
(At least 'tis thus the stupid peasants told
Their wide-mouth'd wives when they the tale unroll'd.)
The village wonder'd why De Blois had kept
His spouse's loss unmention'd and unwept,
Nor were there lacking sland'rous tongues to claim
That the dark master was himself to blame.
But village talk could scarcely hope to solve
A crime so deep, and thus the months revolve:
The rural train repeat the gruesome tale,
And gape and marvel more than they bewail.

Swift flew the sun, and winter once again
With icy talons gripp'd the frigid plain.
December brought its store of Christmas cheer,

And grateful peasants hail'd the op'ning year;
But by the hearth as Candlemas drew nigh,
The whisp'ring ancients spoke of things gone by.
Few had forgot the dark demoniac lore
Of things that came the Candlemas before,
And many a crone intently eyed the house
Where dwelt the sadden'd bailiff and his spouse.
At last the day arriv'd, the sky o'erspread
With dark'ning messengers and clouds of lead;
Each neighb'ring grove Aeolian warnings sigh'd,
And thick'ning terrors broadcast seem'd to bide.
The good folk, tho' they knew not why, would run
Swift past the bailiff's door, the scene to shun;
Within the house the grieving couple wept,
And mourn'd the child who now forever slept.
On rush'd the dusk in doubly hideous form,
Borne on the pinions of the gath'ring storm;
Unusual murmurs fill'd the rainless wind,
The rising river lash'd the troubled shore;
Black thro' the night the awful storm-god prowl'd,
And froze the list'ners' life-blood as he howl'd;
Gigantic trees like supple rushes sway'd,
Whilst for his home the trembling cotter pray'd.

Now falls a sudden lull amidst the gale;
With less'ning force the circling currents wail;
Far down the stream that laves the neighb'ring mead
Burst a new ululation, wildly key'd;
The peasant train a frantic mien assume,
And huddle closer in the spectral gloom:
To each strain'd ear the truth too well is known,

27

For that dread sound can come from wolves alone!
The rustics close attend, when ere they think,
A lupine army swarms the river's brink;
From out the waters leap a howling train
That rend the air, and scatter o'er the plain:
With flaming orbs the frothing creatures fly,
And chant with hellish voice their hungry cry.
First of the pack a mighty monster leaps
With fearless tread, and martial order keeps;
Th' attendant wolves his yelping tones obey,
And form in columns for the coming fray:
No frighten'd swain they harm, but silent bound
With a fix'd purpose o'er the frozen ground.
Straight course the monsters thro' the village street,
Unholy vigour in their flying feet;
Thro' half-shut blinds the shelter'd peasants peer,
And wax in wonder as they lose in fear.
Th' excited pack at last their goal perceive,
And the vex'd air with deaf'ning clamour cleave;
The churls, astonish'd, watch th' unnatural herd
Flock round a cottage at the leader's word:
Quick spreads the fearsome fact, by rumour blown,
That the doom'd cottage is the bailiff's own!

Round and around the howling daemons glide,
Whilst the fierce leader scales the vine-clad side;
The frantic wind its horrid wail renews,
And mutters madly thro' the lifeless yews.
In the frail house the bailiff calmly waits
The rav'ning horde, and trusts th' impartial Fates,
But the wan wife revives with curious mien

Another monster and an older scene;
Amidst th' increasing wind that rocks the walls,
The dame to him the serpent's deed recalls:
Then as a nameless thought fills both their minds,
The bare-fang'd leader crashes thro' the blinds.
Across the room, with murd'rous fury rife,
Leaps the mad wolf, and seizes on the wife;
With strange intent he drags his shrieking prey
Close to the spot where once the coffin lay.
Wilder and wilder roars the mounting gale
That sweeps the hills and hurtles thro' the vale;
The ill-made cottage shakes, the pack without
Dance with new fury in demoniac rout.

Quick as his thought, the valiant bailiff stands
Above the wolf, a weapon in his hands;
The ready axe that serv'd a year before,
Now serves as well to slay one monster more.
The creature drops inert, with shatter'd head,
Full on the floor, and silent as the dead;
The rescu'd wife recalls the dire alarms,
And faints from terror in her husband's arms.
But as he holds her, all the cottage quakes,
And with full force the titan tempest breaks:
Down crash the walls, and o'er their shrinking forms
Burst the mad revels of the storm of storms.
Th' encircling wolves advance with ghastly pace,
Hunger and murder in each gleaming face,
But as they close, from out the hideous night
Flashes a bolt of unexpected light:
The vivid scene to ev'ry eye appears,

And peasants shiver with returning fears.
Above the wreck the scatheless chimney stays,
Its outline glimm'ring in the fitful rays,
Whilst o'er the hearth still hangs the household shrine,
The Saviour's image and the Cross divine!
Round the blest spot a lambent radiance glows,
And shields the cotters from their stealthy foes:
Each monstrous creature marks the wondrous glare,
Drops, fades, and vanishes in empty air!
The village train with startled eyes adore,
And count their beads in rev'rence o'er and o'er.
Now fades the light, and dies the raging blast,
The hour of dread and reign of horror past.
Pallid and bruis'd, from out his toppled walls
The panting bailiff with his good wife crawls:
Kind hands attend them, whilst o'er all the town
A strange sweet peace of spirit settles down.
Wonder and fear are still'd in soothing sleep,
As thro' the breaking clouds the moon rays peep.

Here paus'd the prattling grandam in her speech,
Confus'd with age, the tale half out of reach;
The list'ning guest, impatient for a clue,
Fears 'tis not one tale, but a blend of two;
He fain would know how far'd the widow'd lord
Whose eerie ways th' initial theme afford,
And marvels that the crone so quick should slight
His fate, to babble of the wolf-wrack'd night.
The old wife, press'd, for greater clearness strives,
Nods wisely, and her scatter'd wits revives;
Yet strangely lingers on her latter tale

Of wolf and bailiff, miracle and gale.
When (quoth the crone) the dawn's bright radiance bath'd
Th' eventful scene, so late in terror swath'd,
The chatt'ring churls that sought the ruin'd cot
Found a new marvel in the gruesome spot.
From fallen walls a trail of gory red,
As of the stricken wolf, erratic led;
O'er road and mead the new-dript crimson wound,
Till lost amidst the neighb'ring swampy ground:
With wonder unappeas'd the peasants burn'd,
For what the quicksand takes is ne'er return'd.

Once more the grandam, with a knowing eye,
Stops in her tale, to watch a hawk soar by;
The weary list'ner, baffled, seeks anew
For some plain statement, or enlight'ning clue.
Th' indulgent crone attends the puzzled plea,
Yet strangely mutters o'er the mystery.
The Sieur? Ah, yes—that morning all in vain
His shaking servants scour'd the frozen plain;
No man had seen him since he rode away
In silence on the dark preceding day.
His horse, wild-eyed with some unusual fright,
Came wand'ring from the river-bank that night.
His hunting-hound, that mourn'd with piteous woe,
Howl'd by the quicksand swamp, his grief to shew.
The village folk thought much, but utter'd less;
The servants' search wore out in emptiness:
For Sieur De Blois (the old wife's tale is o'er)
Was lost to mortal sight for evermore.

Part II.

The 1929-1930 Resurgence.

The centerpiece of the poetry in this volume, including *Fungi from Yuggoth*, dates from a very narrow span of time, covering just a little more than a month from late November 1929 to very early January 1930.

Lovecraft's return to a serious pursuit of poetry started with a small flurry of poems written in November 1929—the burst of output that culminated in *Fungi from Yuggoth*. It started, more or less, with two poems apparently crafted on the same day—November 26, 1929: *The Outpost*, and *The Ancient Track*— which follow:

The Outpost.

When evening cools the yellow stream,
And shadows stalk the jungle's ways,
Zimbabwe's palace flares ablaze
For a great King who fears to dream.

For he alone of all mankind
Waded the swamp that serpents shun;
And struggling toward the setting sun,
Came on the veldt that lies behind.

No other eyes had vented there
Since eyes were lent for human sight—
But there, as sunset turned to night,
He found the Elder Secret's lair.

Strange turrets rose beyond the plain,
And walls and bastions spread around
The distant domes that fouled the ground
Like leprous fungi after rain.

A grudging moon writhed up to shine
Past leagues where life can have no home;
And paling far-off tower and dome,
Shewed each unwindowed and malign.

Then he who in his boyhood ran
Through vine-hung ruins free of fear,
Trembled at what he saw—for here
Was no dead, ruined seat of man.

Inhuman shapes, half-seen, half-guessed,
Half solid and half ether-spawned,
Seethed down from starless voids that yawned
In heav'n, to these blank walls of pest.

And voidward from that pest-mad zone
Amorphous hordes seethed darkly back,
Their dim claws laden with the wrack
Of things that men have dreamed and known.

The ancient Fishers from Outside—
Were there not tales the high-priest told,
Of how they found the worlds of old,
And took what pelf their fancy spied?

Their hidden, dread-ringed outposts brood
Upon a million worlds of space;
Abhorred by every living race,
Yet scatheless in their solitude.

Sweating with fright, the watcher crept
Back to the swamp that serpents shun,
So that he lay, by rise of sun,
Safe in the palace where he slept.

None saw him leave, or come at dawn,
Nor does his flesh bear any mark
Of what he met in that curs't dark—
Yet from his sleep all peace has gone.

When evening cools the yellow stream,
And shadows stalk the jungle's ways,
Zimbabwe's palace flares ablaze,
For a great King who fears to dream.

The Ancient Track.

There was no hand to hold me back
That night I found the ancient track
Over the hill, and strained to see
The fields that teased my memory.
This tree, that wall—I knew them well,
And all the roofs and orchards fell
Familiarly upon my mind
As from a past not far behind.
I knew what shadows would be cast
When the late moon came up at last
From back of Zaman's Hill, and how
The vale would shine three hours from now.
And when the path grew steep and high,
And seemed to end against the sky,
I had no fear of what might rest

Beyond that silhouetted crest.
Straight on I walked, while all the night
Grew pale with phosphorescent light,
And wall and farmhouse gable glowed
Unearthly by the climbing road.
There was the milestone that I knew—
"Two miles to Dunwich"—now the view
Of distant spire and roofs would dawn
With ten more upward paces gone....

There was no hand to hold me back
That night I found the ancient track,
And reached the crest to see outspread
A valley of the lost and dead:
And over Zaman's Hill the horn
Of a malignant moon was born,
To light the weeds and vines that grew
On ruined walls I never knew.
The fox-fire glowed in field and bog,
And unknown waters spewed a fog
Whose curling talons mocked the thought
That I had ever known this spot.
Too well I saw from the mad scene
That my loved past had never been—
Nor was I now upon the trail
Descending to that long-dead vale.
Around was fog—ahead, the spray
Of star-streams in the Milky Way....

There was no hand to hold me back
That night I found the ancient track.

Part III.

Fungi from Yuggoth.

We now reach Lovecraft's poetic *chef d'oeuvre*, and the titular work of this collection: *Fungi from Yuggoth*.

Fungi from Yuggoth is a collection of sonnets in several different styles. I'm going to take about two minutes of your time to explain the difference, because it will affect your enjoyment of the poems.

The majority of them are in the Petrarchan form, in which the rhyme scheme of the first eight lines is A-B-B-A A-B-B-A—a very difficult form to work with in English, although easier in Italian. (Actually, the majority of the sonnets here—19 of the 36, all told—are in a modified Petrarchan form, an A-B-B-A C-D-D-C arrangement, which is, of course, considerably easier to manage in either English or Italian.)

Sonnets 1, 4, 5, 8, 9, 11-14, 16-21 and 22-36 are in the

Petrarchan or modified Petrarchan form. Petrarchan sonnets typically finish with a sestet, usually C-D-C-D-C-D, but Lovecraft was far too well tuned to the dramatic power of a final couplet to fall for that one. His final sestets invariably finish with a couplet, just like in the Shakespearean sonnets that also appear in *Fungi from Yuggoth*.

Sonnets 2, 3, 6, 7, 10, 15, 22 and 23 are in the Shakespearean form. The Shakespearean sonnet format is more familiar to most English-speaking casual poetry readers, because, of course, of the Shakespearean sonnets themselves. The rhyme scheme for these is A-B-A-B, C-D-C-D, E-F-E-F, G-G—a much easier scheme to fit words to in English.

You may have noticed an interesting fact: Not only are there far more of the tougher Petrarchan sonnets in *Fungi from Yuggoth*, but the number of easy Shakespearean ones dwindles as the cycle proceeds, until after Sonnet 15, only one of the final 16 poems is in that form. It appears that Lovecraft was getting into the groove of the work, and increasingly reluctant to settle for the easier form as time and poems went by.

Let's now turn to the first of Lovecraft's sonnets in the *Fungi from Yuggoth* cycle.

I.

The Book.

The place was dark and dusty and half-lost
In tangles of old alleys near the quays,
Reeking of strange things brought in from the seas,
And with queer curls of fog that west winds tossed.
Small lozenge panes, obscured by smoke and frost,
Just shewed the books, in piles like twisted trees,
Rotting from floor to roof—congeries
Of crumbling elder lore at little cost.
I entered, charmed, and from a cobwebbed heap
Took up the nearest tome and thumbed it through,
Trembling at curious words that seemed to keep
Some secret, monstrous if one only knew.
Then, looking for some seller old in craft,
I could find nothing but a voice that laughed.

II.

Pursuit.

I held the book beneath my coat, at pains
To hide the thing from sight in such a place;
Hurrying through the ancient harbor lanes
With often-turning head and nervous pace.
Dull, furtive windows in old tottering brick
Peered at me oddly as I hastened by,
And thinking what they sheltered, I grew sick
For a redeeming glimpse of clean blue sky.
No one had seen me take the thing—but still
A blank laugh echoed in my whirling head,
And I could guess what nighted worlds of ill
Lurked in that volume I had coveted.
The way grew strange—the walls alike and madding—
And far behind me, unseen feet were padding.

III.

The Key.

I do not know what windings in the waste
Of those strange sea-lanes brought me home once more,
But on my porch I trembled, white with haste
To get inside and bolt the heavy door.
I had the book that told the hidden way
Across the void and through the space-hung screens
That hold the undimensioned worlds at bay,
And keep lost aeons to their own demesnes.
At last the key was mine to those vague visions
Of sunset spires and twilight woods that brood
Dim in the gulfs beyond this earth's precisions,
Lurking as memories of infinitude.
The key was mine, but as I sat there mumbling,
The attic window shook with a faint fumbling.

IV.

Recognition.

The day had come again, when as a child
I saw—just once—that hollow of old oaks,
Grey with a ground-mist that enfolds and chokes
The slinking shapes which madness has defiled.
It was the same—an herbage rank and wild
Clings round an altar whose carved sign invokes
That Nameless One to whom a thousand smokes
Rose, aeons gone, from unclean towers up-piled.
I saw the body spread on that dank stone,
And knew those things which feasted were not men;
I knew this strange, grey world was not my own,
But Yuggoth, past the starry voids—and then
The body shrieked at me with a dead cry,
And all too late I knew that it was I!

V.

Homecoming.

The daemon said that he would take me home
To the pale, shadowy land I half recalled
As a high place of stair and terrace, walled
With marble balustrades that sky-winds comb,
While miles below a maze of dome on dome
And tower on tower beside a sea lies sprawled.
Once more, he told me, I would stand enthralled
On those old heights, and hear the far-off foam.
All this he promised, and through sunset's gate
He swept me, past the lapping lakes of flame,
And red-gold thrones of gods without a name
Who shriek in fear at some impending fate.
Then a black gulf with sea-sounds in the night:
"Here was your home," he mocked, "when you had sight!"

VI.

The Lamp.

We found the lamp inside those hollow cliffs
Whose chiseled sign no priest in Thebes could read,
And from whose caverns frightened hieroglyphs
Warned every living creature of earth's breed.
No more was there—just that one brazen bowl
With traces of a curious oil within;
Fretted with some obscurely patterned scroll,
And symbols hinting vaguely of strange sin.
Little the fears of forty centuries meant
To us as we bore off our slender spoil,
And when we scanned it in our darkened tent
We struck a match to test the ancient oil.
It blazed—great God!... But the vast shapes we saw
In that mad flash have seared our lives with awe.

VII.

Zaman's Hill.

The great hill hung close over the old town,
A precipice against the main street's end;
Green, tall, and wooded, looking darkly down
Upon the steeple at the highway bend.
Two hundred years the whispers had been heard
About what happened on the man-shunned slope—
Tales of an oddly mangled deer or bird,
Or of lost boys whose kin had ceased to hope.
One day the mail-man found no village there,
Nor were its folk or houses seen again;
People came out from Aylesbury to stare—
Yet they all told the mail-man it was plain
That he was mad for saying he had spied
The great hill's gluttonous eyes, and jaws stretched wide.

VIII.

The Port.

Ten miles from Arkham I had struck the trail
That rides the cliff-edge over Boynton Beach,
And hoped that just at sunset I could reach
The crest that looks on Innsmouth in the vale.
Far out at sea was a retreating sail,
White as hard years of ancient winds could bleach,
But evil with some portent beyond speech,
So that I did not wave my hand or hail.
Sails out of Innsmouth! echoing old renown
Of long-dead times. But now a too-swift night
Is closing in, and I have reached the height
Whence I so often scan the distant town.
The spires and roofs are there—but look! The gloom
Sinks on dark lanes, as lightless as the tomb!

IX.

The Courtyard.

It was the city I had known before;
The ancient, leprous town where mongrel throngs
Chant to strange gods, and beat unhallowed gongs
In crypts beneath foul alleys near the shore.
The rotting, fish-eyed houses leered at me
From where they leaned, drunk and half-animate,
As edging through the filth I passed the gate
To the black courtyard where the man would be.
The dark walls closed me in, and loud I cursed
That ever I had come to such a den,
When suddenly a score of windows burst
Into wild light, and swarmed with dancing men:
Mad, soundless revels of the dragging dead—
And not a corpse had either hands or head!

X.

The Pigeon-Flyers.

They took me slumming, where gaunt walls of brick
Bulge outward with a viscous stored-up evil,
And twisted faces, thronging foul and thick,
Wink messages to alien god and devil.
A million fires were blazing in the streets,
And from flat roofs a furtive few would fly
Bedraggled birds into the yawning sky
While hidden drums droned on with measured beats.
I knew those fires were brewing monstrous things,
And that those birds of space had been Outside—
I guessed to what dark planet's crypts they plied,
And what they brought from Thog beneath their wings.
The others laughed—till struck too mute to speak
By what they glimpsed in one bird's evil beak.

XI.

The Well.

Farmer Seth Atwood was past eighty when
He tried to sink that deep well by his door,
With only Eb to help him bore and bore.
We laughed, and hoped he'd soon be sane again.
And yet, instead, young Eb went crazy, too,
So that they shipped him to the county farm.
Seth bricked the well-mouth up as tight as glue—
Then hacked an artery in his gnarled left arm.
After the funeral we felt bound to get
Out to that well and rip the bricks away,
But all we saw were iron hand-holds set
Down a black hole deeper than we could say.
And yet we put the bricks back—for we found
The hole too deep for any line to sound.

XII.

The Howler.

They told me not to take the Briggs' Hill path
That used to be the highroad through to Zoar,
For Goody Watkins, hanged in seventeen-four,
Had left a certain monstrous aftermath.
Yet when I disobeyed, and had in view
The vine-hung cottage by the great rock slope,
I could not think of elms or hempen rope,
But wondered why the house still seemed so new.
Stopping a while to watch the fading day,
I heard faint howls, as from a room upstairs,
When through the ivied panes one sunset ray
Struck in, and caught the howler unawares.
I glimpsed—and ran in frenzy from the place,
And from a four-pawed thing with human face.

XIII.

Hesperia.

The winter sunset, flaming beyond spires
And chimneys half-detached from this dull sphere,
Opens great gates to some forgotten year
Of elder splendours and divine desires.
Expectant wonders burn in those rich fires,
Adventure-fraught, and not untinged with fear;
A row of sphinxes where the way leads clear
Toward walls and turrets quivering to far lyres.
It is the land where beauty's meaning flowers;
Where every unplaced memory has a source;
Where the great river Time begins its course
Down the vast void in starlit streams of hours.
Dreams bring us close—but ancient lore repeats
That human tread has never soiled these streets.

XIV.

Star-Winds.

It is a certain hour of twilight glooms,
Mostly in autumn, when the star-wind pours
Down hilltop streets, deserted out-of-doors,
But shewing early lamplight from snug rooms.
The dead leaves rush in strange, fantastic twists,
And chimney-smoke whirls round with alien grace,
Heeding geometries of outer space,
While Fomalhaut peers in through southward mists.
This is the hour when moonstruck poets know
What fungi sprout in Yuggoth, and what scents
And tints of flowers fill Nithon's continents,
Such as in no poor earthly garden blow.
Yet for each dream these winds to us convey,
A dozen more of ours they sweep away!

XV.

Antarktos.

Deep in my dream the great bird whispered queerly
Of the black cone amid the polar waste;
Pushing above the ice-sheet lone and drearly,
By storm-crazed aeons battered and defaced.
Hither no living earth-shapes take their courses,
And only pale auroras and faint suns
Glow on that pitted rock, whose primal sources
Are guessed at dimly by the Elder Ones.
If men should glimpse it, they would merely wonder
What tricky mound of Nature's build they spied;
But the bird told of vaster parts, that under
The mile-deep ice-shroud crouch and brood and bide.
God help the dreamer whose mad visions shew
Those dead eyes set in crystal gulfs below!

XVI.

The Window.

The house was old, with tangled wings outthrown,
Of which no one could ever half keep track,
And in a small room somewhat near the back
Was an odd window sealed with ancient stone.
There, in a dream-plagued childhood, quite alone
I used to go, where night reigned vague and black;
Parting the cobwebs with a curious lack
Of fear, and with a wonder each time grown.
One later day I brought the masons there
To find what view my dim forbears had shunned,
But as they pierced the stone, a rush of air
Burst from the alien voids that yawned beyond.
They fled—but I peered through and found unrolled
All the wild worlds of which my dreams had told.

XVII.

A Memory.

There were great steppes, and rocky table-lands
Stretching half-limitless in starlit night,
With alien campfires shedding feeble light
On beasts with tinkling bells, in shaggy bands.
Far to the south the plain sloped low and wide
To a dark zigzag line of wall that lay
Like a huge python of some primal day
Which endless time had chilled and petrified.
I shivered oddly in the cold, thin air,
And wondered where I was and how I came,
When a cloaked form against a campfire's glare
Rose and approached, and called me by my name.
Staring at that dead face beneath the hood,
I ceased to hope—because I understood.

XVIII.

The Gardens of Yin.

Beyond that wall, whose ancient masonry
Reached almost to the sky in moss-thick towers,
There would be terraced gardens, rich with flowers,
And flutter of bird and butterfly and bee.
There would be walks, and bridges arching over
Warm lotos-pools reflecting temple eaves,
And cherry-trees with delicate boughs and leaves
Against a pink sky where the herons hover.
All would be there, for had not old dreams flung
Open the gate to that stone-lanterned maze
Where drowsy streams spin out their winding ways,
Trailed by green vines from bending branches hung?
I hurried—but when the wall rose, grim and great,
I found there was no longer any gate.

XIX.

The Bells.

Year after year I heard that faint, far ringing
Of deep-toned bells on the black midnight wind;
Peals from no steeple I could ever find,
But strange, as if across some great void winging.
I searched my dreams and memories for a clue,
And thought of all the chimes my visions carried;
Of quiet Innsmouth, where the white gulls tarried
Around an ancient spire that once I knew.
Always perplexed I heard those far notes falling,
Till one March night the bleak rain splashing cold
Beckoned me back through gateways of recalling
To elder towers where the mad clappers tolled.
They tolled—but from the sunless tides that pour
Through sunken valleys on the sea's dead floor.

XX.

Night-Gaunts.

Out of what crypt they crawl, I cannot tell,
But every night I see the rubbery things,
Black, horned, and slender, with membraneous wings,
And tails that bear the bifid barb of hell.
They come in legions on the north wind's swell,
With obscene clutch that titillates and stings,
Snatching me off on monstrous voyagings
To grey worlds hidden deep in nightmare's well.
Over the jagged peaks of Thok they sweep,
Heedless of all the cries I try to make,
And down the nether pits to that foul lake
Where the puffed shoggoths splash in doubtful sleep.
But oh! If only they would make some sound,
Or wear a face where faces should be found!

XXI.

Nyarlathotep.

And at the last from inner Egypt came
The strange dark One to whom the fellahs bowed;
Silent and lean and cryptically proud,
And wrapped in fabrics red as sunset flame.
Throngs pressed around, frantic for his commands,
But leaving, could not tell what they had heard;
While through the nations spread the awestruck word
That wild beasts followed him and licked his hands.
Soon from the sea a noxious birth began;
Forgotten lands with weedy spires of gold;
The ground was cleft, and mad auroras rolled
Down on the quaking citadels of man.
Then, crushing what he chanced to mould in play,
The idiot Chaos blew Earth's dust away.

XXII.

Azathoth.

Out in the mindless void the daemon bore me,
Past the bright clusters of dimensioned space,
Till neither time nor matter stretched before me,
But only Chaos, without form or place.
Here the vast Lord of All in darkness muttered
Things he had dreamed but could not understand,
While near him shapeless bat-things flopped and fluttered
In idiot vortices that ray-streams fanned.
They danced insanely to the high, thin whining
Of a cracked flute clutched in a monstrous paw,
Whence flow the aimless waves whose chance combining
Gives each frail cosmos its eternal law.
"I am His Messenger," the daemon said,
As in contempt he struck his Master's head.

XXIII.

Mirage.

I do not know if ever it existed—
That lost world floating dimly on Time's stream—
And yet I see it often, violet-misted,
And shimmering at the back of some vague dream.
There were strange towers and curious lapping rivers,
Labyrinths of wonder, and low vaults of light,
And bough-crossed skies of flame, like that which quivers
Wistfully just before a winter's night.
Great moors led off to sedgy shores unpeopled,
Where vast birds wheeled, while on a windswept hill
There was a village, ancient and white-steepled,
With evening chimes for which I listen still.
I do not know what land it is—or dare
Ask when or why I was, or will be, there.

XXIV.

The Canal.

Somewhere in dream there is an evil place
Where tall, deserted buildings crowd along
A deep, black, narrow channel, reeking strong
Of frightful things whence oily currents race.
Lanes with old walls half meeting overhead
Wind off to streets one may or may not know,
And feeble moonlight sheds a spectral glow
Over long rows of windows, dark and dead.
There are no footfalls, and the one soft sound
Is of the oily water as it glides
Under stone bridges, and along the sides
Of its deep flume, to some vague ocean bound.
None lives to tell when that stream washed away
Its dream-lost region from the world of clay.

XXV.

St. Toad's.

"Beware St. Toad's cracked chimes!" I heard him scream
As I plunged into those mad lanes that wind
In labyrinths obscure and undefined
South of the river where old centuries dream.
He was a furtive figure, bent and ragged,
And in a flash had staggered out of sight,
So still I burrowed onward in the night
Toward where more roof-lines rose, malign and jagged.
No guide-book told of what was lurking here—
But now I heard another old man shriek:
"Beware St. Toad's cracked chimes!" And growing weak,
I paused, when a third greybeard croaked in fear:
"Beware St. Toad's cracked chimes!" Aghast, I fled—
Till suddenly that black spire loomed ahead.

XXVI.

The Familiars.

John Whateley lived about a mile from town,
Up where the hills begin to huddle thick;
We never thought his wits were very quick,
Seeing the way he let his farm run down.
He used to waste his time on some queer books
He'd found around the attic of his place,
Till funny lines got creased into his face,
And folks all said they didn't like his looks.
When he began those night-howls we declared
He'd better be locked up away from harm,
So three men from the Aylesbury town farm
Went for him—but came back alone and scared.
They'd found him talking to two crouching things
That at their step flew off on great black wings.

XXVII.

The Elder Pharos.

From Leng, where rocky peaks climb bleak and bare
Under cold stars obscure to human sight,
There shoots at dusk a single beam of light
Whose far blue rays make shepherds whine in prayer.
They say (though none has been there) that it comes
Out of a pharos in a tower of stone,
Where the last Elder One lives on alone,
Talking to Chaos with the beat of drums.
The Thing, they whisper, wears a silken mask
Of yellow, whose queer folds appear to hide
A face not of this earth, though none dares ask
Just what those features are, which bulge inside.
Many, in man's first youth, sought out that glow,
But what they found, no one will ever know.

XXVIII.

Expectancy.

I cannot tell why some things hold for me
A sense of unplumbed marvels to befall,
Or of a rift in the horizon's wall
Opening to worlds where only gods can be.
There is a breathless, vague expectancy,
As of vast ancient pomps I half recall,
Or wild adventures, uncorporeal,
Ecstasy-fraught, and as a day-dream free.
It is in sunsets and strange city spires,
Old villages and woods and misty downs,
South winds, the sea, low hills, and lighted towns,
Old gardens, half-heard songs, and the moon's fires.
But though its lure alone makes life worth living,
None gains or guesses what it hints at giving.

XXIX.

Nostalgia.

Once every year, in autumn's wistful glow,
The birds fly out over an ocean waste,
Calling and chattering in a joyous haste
To reach some land their inner memories know.
Great terraced gardens where bright blossoms blow,
And lines of mangoes luscious to the taste,
And temple-groves with branches interlaced
Over cool paths—all these their vague dreams shew.
They search the sea for marks of their old shore—
For the tall city, white and turreted—
But only empty waters stretch ahead,
So that at last they turn away once more.
Yet sunken deep where alien polyps throng,
The old towers miss their lost, remembered song.

XXX.

Background.

I never can be tied to raw, new things,
For I first saw the light in an old town,
Where from my window huddled roofs sloped down
To a quaint harbour rich with visionings.
Streets with carved doorways where the sunset beams
Flooded old fanlights and small window-panes,
And Georgian steeples topped with gilded vanes—
These were the sights that shaped my childhood dreams.
Such treasures, left from times of cautious leaven,
Cannot but loose the hold of flimsier wraiths
That flit with shifting ways and muddled faiths
Across the changeless walls of earth and heaven.
They cut the moment's thongs and leave me free
To stand alone before eternity.

XXXI.

The Dweller.

It had been old when Babylon was new;
None knows how long it slept beneath that mound,
Where in the end our questing shovels found
Its granite blocks and brought it back to view.
There were vast pavements and foundation-walls,
And crumbling slabs and statues, carved to shew
Fantastic beings of some long ago
Past anything the world of man recalls.
And then we saw those stone steps leading down
Through a choked gate of graven dolomite
To some black haven of eternal night
Where elder signs and primal secrets frown.
We cleared a path—but raced in mad retreat
When from below we heard those clumping feet.

XXXII.

Alienation.

His solid flesh had never been away,
For each dawn found him in his usual place,
But every night his spirit loved to race
Through gulfs and worlds remote from common day.
He had seen Yaddith, yet retained his mind,
And come back safely from the Ghooric zone,
When one still night across curved space was thrown
That beckoning piping from the voids behind.
He waked that morning as an older man,
And nothing since has looked the same to him.
Objects around float nebulous and dim—
False, phantom trifles of some vaster plan.
His folk and friends are now an alien throng
To which he struggles vainly to belong.

XXXIII.

Harbour Whistles.

Over old roofs and past decaying spires
The harbour whistles chant all through the night;
Throats from strange ports, and beaches far and white,
And fabulous oceans, ranged in motley choirs.
Each to the other alien and unknown,
Yet all, by some obscurely focussed force
From brooding gulfs beyond the Zodiac's course,
Fused into one mysterious cosmic drone.
Through shadowy dreams they send a marching line
Of still more shadowy shapes and hints and views;
Echoes from outer voids, and subtle clues
To things which they themselves cannot define.
And always in that chorus, faintly blent,
We catch some notes no earth-ship ever sent.

XXXIV.

Recapture.

The way led down a dark, half-wooded heath
Where moss-grey boulders humped above the mould,
And curious drops, disquieting and cold,
Sprayed up from unseen streams in gulfs beneath.
There was no wind, nor any trace of sound
In puzzling shrub, or alien-featured tree,
Nor any view before—till suddenly,
Straight in my path, I saw a monstrous mound.
Half to the sky those steep sides loomed upspread,
Rank-grassed, and cluttered by a crumbling flight
Of lava stairs that scaled the fear-topped height
In steps too vast for any human tread.
I shrieked—and knew what primal star and year
Had sucked me back from man's dream-transient sphere!

XXXV.

Evening Star.

I saw it from that hidden, silent place
Where the old wood half shuts the meadow in.
It shone through all the sunset's glories—thin
At first, but with a slowly brightening face.
Night came, and that lone beacon, amber-hued,
Beat on my sight as never it did of old;
The evening star—but grown a thousandfold
More haunting in this hush and solitude.
It traced strange pictures on the quivering air—
Half-memories that had always filled my eyes—
Vast towers and gardens; curious seas and skies
Of some dim life—I never could tell where.
But now I knew that through the cosmic dome
Those rays were calling from my far, lost home.

XXXVI.

Continuity.

There is in certain ancient things a trace
Of some dim essence—more than form or weight;
A tenuous aether, indeterminate,
Yet linked with all the laws of time and space.
A faint, veiled sign of continuities
That outward eyes can never quite descry;
Of locked dimensions harbouring years gone by,
And out of reach except for hidden keys.
It moves me most when slanting sunbeams glow
On old farm buildings set against a hill,
And paint with life the shapes which linger still
From centuries less a dream than this we know.
In that strange light I feel I am not far
From the fixt mass whose sides the ages are.

Part IV.

Late poetry: 1935-1936.

The seven years Lovecraft lived after he finished *Fungi from Yuggoth* were full and productive ones— if somewhat lean and hungry. Faced with a progressively more and more straitened budget, Lovecraft lived on beans, cheese and bread to conserve his capital—saving up for bus and train fare for the extensive travels he engaged in most summers. Off his ever-prolific pen flowed hundreds of thousands of words during those years, mostly in the form of letters and the extensive travelogues with which he was wont to finish up each year's journeys.

It was also during this time that he wrote the weird fiction that most consider to be the best work of his life, including *The Whisperer in Darkness*, *At the Mountains of Madness*, *The Dreams in the Witch-House*, and *The Shadow out of Time*.

But after 1930, very little of what Lovecraft wrote was poetry, and what little poetry he did write was quite short.

The two examples that we have provided, both penned in 1936, are on the long side of his 1930s output. Interestingly, both of them are sonnets.

In a Sequester'd Providence Churchyard
Where Once Poe Walk'd.

Eternal brood the shadows on this ground,
Dreaming of centuries that have gone before;
Great elms rise solemnly by slab and mound,
Arch'd high above a hidden world of yore.
Round all the scene a light of memory plays,
And dead leaves whisper of departed days,
Longing for sights and sounds that are no more.

Lonely and sad, a spectre glides along
Aisles where of old his living footsteps fell;
No common glance discerns him, tho' his song
Peals down thro' time with a mysterious spell:
Only the few who sorcery's secret know
Espy amidst these tombs the shade of Poe.

To Clark Ashton Smith, Esq., upon His Phantastick Tales, Verses, Pictures, and Sculptures.

A time-black tower against dim banks of cloud;
Around its base the pathless, pressing wood.
Shadow and silence, moss and mould, enshroud
Grey, age-fell'd slabs that once as cromlechs stood.
No fall of foot, no song of bird awakes
The lethal aisles of sempiternal night,
Tho' oft with stir of wings the dense air shakes,
As in the tower there glows a pallid light.

For here, apart, dwells one whose hands have wrought
Strange eidola that chill the world with fear;
Whose graven runes in tones of dread have taught

What things beyond the star-gulfs lurk and leer.
Dark Lord of Averoigne—whose windows stare
On pits of dream no other gaze could bear!

Other Pulp-Lit Annotated Editions by H.P. Lovecraft:

H.P. LOVECRAFT: The Complete Omnibus, Vol. I: 1917-1926:

- Hardcover (558 pages)
- Pulp-sized 7x10 softcover
- E-book
- Audiobook (23.5 hours)

H.P. LOVECRAFT: The Complete Omnibus, Vol. II: 1927-1935:

- Hardcover (606 pages)
- Pulp-sized 7x10 softcover
- E-book
- Audiobook (27 hours)

SUPERNATURAL HORROR IN LITERATURE by H.P. Lovecraft.

- Hardcover (128 pages)
- Pocket-size softcover
- E-book
- Audiobook (3 hours)

For a full catalog search "Pulp-Lit" on your favorite bookseller's Website, or see **http://pulp-lit.com.**

CPSIA information can be obtained
at www.ICGtesting.com
Printed in the USA
LVHW021538050721
691891LV00017B/928